THE WAY AROUND

THE WAY AROUND

A Pretentious Collection of Very Short Works

by

K.M. Halpern

εpsilon Books

ISBN-13 (paperback): 978-1-945671-02-9

ISBN-13 (ebook): 978-1-945671-03-6

Library of Congress Control Number: 2018914140

Published by Epsilon Books

Printed in the United States of America

Cover Art by Richie Montgomery

First Edition

CONTENTS

The Gasp

A woman gasped.

Why do you gasp, I asked. Has something dramatic happened, has the world stopped spinning, did so-and-so do such-and-such, did the price of ice cream go up?

No, she replied, it just seemed the thing to do.

To do what, I asked.

Why, to do. One must have something to do or one does nothing and has nothing and is nothing.

I could not argue with this. I once had nothing, then I had something. It was sad to lose the nothing, and I still wonder where it went. Is it happy now?

I gasped. It felt good, I was doing something.

She gasped and I gasped and she gasped.

The world could be powered by gasps, I felt the GDP rising, my glory and success assured. They would write on my tombstone: Here lies the greatest gasper.

But no, there was another, greater than I, who had been gasping longer and harder, who had refined the gasp to perfection.

How could I be the greatest gasper if she had done it first and better. If I was a mere student of gasping, a convert, a mentee, a shadow of a speck on her wall.

I gasped, and considered how to remove that obstacle, that She. The woman must have sensed this. She gasped again.

This was too much, I gasped. Neither of us knew how to stop gasping. If I stopped, I would once again be doing nothing and that simply would not do. She gasped too, realizing the dilemma.

I smiled. Her gasps were growing weaker. She would run out of gasps before me. Then I could decide on *her* epitaph. Who better to do so than her student, her convert, the shadow of a speck on her wall.

Here lies a decent gasper, I would write, banishing her to perpetual obscurity. Who would gasp at her greatness then? If her ghost resented me, it would not matter. *I* would be the world's greatest gasper.

But who would write *my* epitaph? If only I could find somebody to hear my gasps before I ran out. Somebody to be my student, my convert, the shadow of a speck on my wall.

A passerby heard me gasp. Why do you gasp, he asked. Has something dramatic happened, has the world started spinning, did such-and-such do so-and-so, did the price of ice cream go down?

No, I replied, it just seemed the thing to do.

Modern Buddha

They gave Buddha a suit, office, paperclips.

"In nothingness we find everything," he began. Someone placed a cup of java in his hand, pushed him into a subway car.

"We wander in unknowing, unseeing, a cloud." The doors opened and he was jostled out.

"I was saying something," he thought as he opened his briefcase for a security guard. One divine light, fading. You can pass.

"There was something on the tip of my tongue..." Come on, you'll be late. someone grabbed his arm, pulled him into the 10 a.m. meeting.

"Something important, I'm on the verge of remembering." Let's go around the table and introduce ourselves. We have a new member of our team. Tell us a little about yourself.

"Hi. I'm Bud. I'll be working in ops."

The Way Around

I began life in the open air, free to wander in any direction. I remember this, but not the feeling.

One day I came across a fence.

I followed it until I reached an opening, which I crossed. How silly, I laughed. How silly to build a fence and leave an opening.

With time, more fences appeared, constraining me to certain paths. There always was an opening, but the way around was long and pointless.

I might have explored the sequestered places, but didn't want to bother finding the entrances. Suppose I entered one and there was no exit, or a new fence barred my return.

The barriers continued to proliferate. Often, there were signs explaining why this or that place was forbidden. Each made sense, promised to be temporary. Over the years, I have never seen a fence removed.

Once, I grew angry and objected. A fence had blocked my favorite path. My friends did not understand.

"Can't you see it is for a good reason," they said. "It's only for a little while." They said I was childish, and turned away.

I determined to protest to the builder of the fences, but could find no one with whom to lodge the complaint.

Inch by inch the fences grew closer, the paths narrower. To no single change could I object. Nobody else seemed to notice.

The day came when one path alone remained, narrow and unpleasant.

We all moved along it, pushed and cursed one another, but never spoke of the fences.

I sometimes wonder about the builder of the fences, what he would say if confronted, whether he is kind or uncaring. Perhaps he regrets erecting them or does not remember.

Does is matter who built these fences? They are here to stay.

Absence

There is no one here, and I do not know why.

Houses stand empty, flags unfurled. The appliances of this age search longingly for masters. There is no damage, no decay.

All is still. Birds do not celebrate the departure of their persecutors, children do not sing in the streets, phones do not ring.

There is no one here, and I do not know why.

Smoke from a campfire rises, languidly wending toward heaven. It finds no conduit, only dissipation. Two silhouettes kneel by the fire. They seem to tend or worship it.

'Hey,' I shout to an absent echo. Then I see them more clearly, instinctively shudder in revulsion. The men's faces are buried in the fire, but no odor sickens me.

The moment passes, yet I linger. Slowly the figures stand. They turn toward me, and are not whole.

There is no one here, and I know why.

The Slide

Here I am, waiting.
For you.
A lost lover you never had.
You will.

You climb the ladder,
so high.
Clamor to get in front
of others.

The slide is long,
and steep.
It goes farther than you thought,
and curves.

It is your turn.
You laugh,
giddy with anticipation,
push off.

It is fun
and fast.
After some time,
you wonder.

You are afraid, try to stop.
You slide.
You scream, call for help.
Nobody comes.

Here I am, waiting.

Twilight

In the morning, my day is filled with possibility. I flit to and fro, consider what to do with the time before me.

What a pity it would be to waste it in unworthy pursuits. Better to choose carefully, the day still is young.

Then it is evening, time is measured. What could I hope to accomplish before I must sleep? Time is to be bided not guarded, too little is left. I dream of what could have been.

And what of the man who thinks he did much with his day? Of the many things which could be, all but one were not. What is the chance he found the right one?

Man with no Name

The other day I met a man with no name, but did not know how to greet him. How does one greet a man with no name? If I said something, others would think I was speaking to them or myself or somebody far far away, unseen but with a name. Perhaps they would strike me or shun me or try to sell me full-term life insurance. That would be unfortunate. I did not wish to be struck or shunned or sold full-term life insurance. I just wanted to speak to the man with no name.

There are many people whose names I do not know. I pass such people all day long, call out to them, and am struck or shunned or sold insurance. But the man with no name is special. It is not that I do not know his name, or that nobody knows his name. He truly has no name. The absence of a name *is* his name, though to put it that way would imply he had a name, which he doesn't. He simply is the man with no name. I would like to ask him how this came to be. How was he born and raised to have no name? But to ask him such things I first would have to greet him, and I do not know how. Perhaps I am greeting him every moment through silence. That seems a reasonable way to greet a man with no name.

I wonder whether his parents had names. One of them must have. There cannot be two people with no name in the world at the same time. Such people would be confused with one another. If everyone confused them, they would be the same person.

What have we, if not a name? Perhaps it is a long name, encompassing the person's full genetics or describing all the atoms in their being. Those names would not be easy to pronounce. I avoid people with such names.

Most sensible people have short names, easily pronounceable names. Names like Bill or Harry or "the first name which cannot be described in twelve words or less." Even "he whose name shall not be spoken" has a name, otherwise what point is there in prohibiting its use? I too have a name, though it is very short and unimpressive. My name is I. It's gauche and lacks punch, but at least I *have* a name.

I do not say this to be snobbish. There is no pecking order, hierarchy, taxonomy of names. There have been many attempts by the sorts of foolish people who do such foolish things. None lasted. Those with undesirably long names replaced them with short ones using new symbols. Those with undesirably short names grew them into long ones.

Most people don't tell me their names. They look away when I ask them, hurry on their way, glancing back furtively. They must be embarrassed of their names, or not know them. It would be a terrible thing not to know your name.

I wonder if the man with no name knows it, or pretends that his name is this or that, something other than nothing. I would like to believe he is at peace with it, and true to form is no man at all.

Dialectic

My friend once announced that he had an idea.

I can prove the world never ends.
Did you know that Mrs. Cribb had her twins taken away?

There can be nothing after the end.
Apparently she had been abusing them because they were favored by her mother.

That includes any thought, any perception.
Where her husband was in all this, nobody knows.

Where thought cannot endure,
there can be no knowledge of the end.
Actually, I suspect it was the elder Cribb who abused them.

If something, by its nature, cannot be known,
it does not meaningfully exist in our mind.
Of course, Mrs. Cribb always was a trollop.

And if it does not exist in any mind — the collective perception of all men, past, present, and future — it has substance only as speculation, unverifiable, irrelevant.
She slept with that Ron fellow too.

If men one day perish, the last will not know
this end, even if he predicts it.
Come to think of it, he may have been the father.

Thus the end contradicts itself, the impossibility of proving the existence of nonexistence.
Sad, really. I suppose that's what happens when your dad's from the South.

With this, the debate concluded.
What happened to my friend, you don't ask?
He died some time ago, choked on a walnut.

A Shattered Symmetry

When first I glimpsed your smile I paused, transfixed. In the mirror's hand lies beauty's secret caress.

Words we had none, the eyes alone minions of seduction.

Perfection's flaw is flaw's absence, and lost in time I could see none.

My heart saw all truth embodied in first vision's hope, an unsustainable optimism.

Without knowing, I discerned a gaping blemish, an affront to sensibility's grace.

So massive this failing, it could not but remain hidden. Only time would ferret it out, and the relaxation of my gaze.

Now you are imperfect, scarred, a final chord misplayed.

I love you even more.

Brum

Derelict dereliction is the new pastime for the rambunctious youth of the effete.

No more burning hobos, killing bums, rousting the homeless, unmanning the unemployed. This is a more refined cruelty.

The gang gathers, clad in chinos and dress shirts, pastel sweaters draped over shoulders, coiffured hair, coiffured smiles, identical boys of identical parents.

They find an unfortunate, sleeping in an alley.
Someone different, someone sad.

A few boys keep watch, make sure nobody happens upon their mischief. When all is ready, they sneak up on the victim, and stand over him, looking down.

Then they do nothing.

Purpose

It is comforting to know your life has no purpose.

If it had a purpose, there is a good chance it would be something demeaning or pointless or tedious. Its only redeeming quality would be that you could point and say, "I have this purpose."

Your purpose could be to pave the way for someone with a greater purpose, to put one tiny stepping stone into place, to be eaten for his amusement, or serve as a cautionary tale.

You could be the jester or the petty crook or any of the cast of minor characters on screen or off screen. There is one hero in a story, and many nobodies.

It could be a bad purpose, a purpose to be ashamed of. Or it could be a great purpose but one you fail to accomplish. Perhaps that failure would be your purpose.

What is the chance your purpose would be something special, something good. That a world which cares nothing for you or equally for all would choose you for greatness, or recognize the greatness already in you. What is the chance the world would not resent you, and instead be moved by envy to assign a purpose unworthy of your greatness?

Isn't it better to have no purpose, for your life to be as meaningless as that of a single blade of grass by the side of the highway.

Not the sort of blade which would inspire such an insight, or any other particular blade that draws your attention. Such blades clearly have purpose. Just *a* blade of grass, generic, unnoticeable and unnoticed. One with no purpose.

It is best to be like that blade of grass, generic, unnoticeable and unnoticed, with no purpose.

Then you can create your own purpose. It would be a fiction to be sure, a repurposing of the word purpose. But all we ever know is someone's fiction. Better your own than another's.

Crossing

I like to walk through fields. There is just grass and me, and the grass always wins. Its scented texture enraptures, enshrouds. How can mere flesh compete?

Wherever I go, I am king. I will outlast each thing I pass, their spans narrowed by man's hand. Every edifice will fail, every tree die, every stone crack. And I do not live long. This is telling.

But I would not spare them, even if I could. They resent me so, resent my freedom, resent my wisdom, resent that they can't resent, They think I am like them, of similar weakness. How arrogant. I will outlast if I cannot outshine.

I like to walk through people. It is a common misconception that they have substance, a less common truth. How else could I get where I need to go? The world is filled with people.

We differ, they and I, these things and people and places. They do not move – each a center, none a part. I circumscribe. The world moves through them, but I move through it. How foolish. A point knows nothing of a line, but a line can see the point.

I like to walk through time, it is inconvenient to do otherwise. What an odd figure, this path. It is mine alone, my dowry to life. No other may point at it and say 'that belongs to me.' From start to end, I alone can trace its contour. It is my proof, my patent.

I flatter myself of its grace, that it boasts obscene geometry, elusive symmetry, an enigma for those who dare try to describe it. Idiots! It took a lifetime to create. Who can hope to unravel its mystery so easily?

Why do I continue to walk? It is hard on the feet, they laugh. Surely it is better to sit or to watch or to sleep. To sleep just a little, surely this can be no sin. I am not convinced. They argue with the wind. There is nobody to convince.

I walk because it is all I may do, all that is given me, the only choice one such as I can have. And they think me a king. Or perhaps a fool. It depends on the they. I wonder what my path looks like. I wonder if it is pretty when seen from afar.

Human Waste

Sixty million calories,
2000 gallons of milk,
15 cows,
4000 chickens,
200 bushels of wheat,
30 tons of fruit and vegetables,
10000 rolls of toilet paper,
200 gallons of soap and shampoo,
1000 tubes of toothpaste,
8 miles of dental floss,
100 tons of refuse,
9 cars,
30 computers,
20 televisions,
80000 gallons of heating oil,
500 megawatt-hours of electricity
from another 25000 gallons of oil,
50000 gallons of gasoline,
a house filled with things,
papers, photos, memories.
All the residue of human existence.
This is what it took to create him,
sustain him.
This is what he took from the world.
What did he give back?
10000 gallons of urine,
8 tons of feces.
He moved boxes for a while,
and then sold fish.

Dissonance

The world hummed in silent harmony. I looked down and saw only good men — pure, wise, incorruptible.

They sought to work together, each striving to do more, demand less. These men could not be tempted or divided. Each beheld his image in the others, and all knew truth.

I put out one's eye, but he was not bitter. I gave one great wealth, and he shared it. I had one slay another, but all thought it an accident.

So I dimmed their vision, made them wear glasses, no two pairs alike. One saw shades of gray, one the left side of things, others only action, inaction, consequence.

Each could discern a fragment of the whole, more divisive this than any chaos of languages. Perceiving and perceived differently, none could be certain of their fellows' motives.

They now fear and distrust one another, each evil in the others' eyes. Yet none has committed any sin.

I look down and see only good men — pure, wise, incorruptible. The world sings in enchanting discord.

Insurance

I wrote a list of all the things I own, in case they are destroyed somehow, and I am not.

If I am destroyed somehow, and they are not, you can have them. To be me you will need nothing more.

Spot

I sit
in a room
in a place
by a thing
on some stuff
near that spot
where something
happened
a while back
to someone
who stood.

Buzz-Saw Bob

People call me Buzz-Saw Bob. That's very convenient. It is good to have a pithy name. A cute, pithy name. Otherwise people would call me Bob. Or Robert. Or that murderous psychopathic bastard. That doesn't sound as cute. It's not alliterative.

If you're tied up in my van, waiting patiently as we drive into the woods, you may be tempted to beg, panic, scream hysterically. It's best not to. Those are things to do when abducted by someone tediously conventional. A Freddy or a Hannibal or a Robert.

Think what fun it will be to tell your friends you were dismembered by Buzz-Saw Bob. They'll all get a good laugh out of it. Who wouldn't want to get dismembered by someone named Buzz-Saw Bob?

It's ok if you can't suppress a chuckle. I won't hold it against you. So cheer up and pipe down. Do you want to end on a down note? Kids these days are so addicted to their phones and pods and TVs, they don't appreciate the small things. Like a funny name.

No need to be nervous. I know it's your first time, but I'm sure you'll do fine. Just relax and I'll take care of everything; I've got lots of experience. Your part will come naturally.

Trust me, you'll make a great story! And think how lucky you are. You could have been murdered by someone named Hack-Saw Harry instead.

Pendulum

We watched the pendulum swing, my friends and I. Some bet it would stay longer on one side or the other, some bet they could will it to change direction.

A few spent whole lives studying the pendulum, seeking to understand why it moved as it did, its motives and weaknesses.

One by one we passed and a new generation of pendulum watchers replaced us, just as eager, just as foolish. But is there anything more worthwhile than pendulum watching? Anything else to pass the time?

The pendulum probably doesn't care. I like to think it will be sad when I die, perhaps swing a little slower just one time.

But I won't bet on it.

Softly

What do you have to say that I possibly wish to hear?

Think it, consider it, turn it over, craft it, refine every detail to perfection, reduce it to its smallest, cleanest pieces, use hammer not chisel, acid not glue.

Once small and clean and elegant beyond compare it still is too long and too loud.

Stop with that primitive squawking. It is an anachronism — inefficient, grating.

How will I hear the delicate sound of truck and jackhammer above your screeching? Do you still fling feces like a monkey? Then don't fling sound.

Write it down, but not as chemicals soaked into dead wood. We've moved past spoiling clay and stone, bark and skin. Why pick and choose?

Modern tools for a modern age. The smallest footprint is of those not born. Soon.

Put it in an email. Then I can delete it, reclaim the valuable space your unthoughts take, use it for something important. Celebrity gossip or bunny photos.

The easier to prove you never were, the better you would have been if you actually were. Be a darling and make it easy to erase you, forget you.

Just unbe.

Place of Honor

You sit with your back to the wall, smug, confident. It is the safest place at the table. Only the most important person can sit there.

But walls have ears, so they must have mouths. What good is listening if they cannot eat?

As we sit here, negotiating, think on this. I have the universe behind me. It has my back. Behind you is the gaping maw of something that never has eaten and is eager for new experiences.

Admonition

Live, Die, Behold! You object? Ah, I see the problem. You have been doing these things in the wrong order. That is why you fear death and love life when you should love death and fear life. What will you behold? Oh, nothing. It is there because three sounds more lyrical than two.

Adult

The adult is a terrible and piteous creature, having forgotten what it is to laugh, to wonder, to hope, lost in the minutiae of the mundane, unaware of its own irrelevance, aware of its own impermanence. Best not to become mutton. Best to remain lamb, tender and true.

Prodigy

I was born with swift legs. Run as fast and as far as they take you, somebody said. So I did, to ever receding cheers, or did they merely diminish?

One day, as field and city passed in a blur, I realized that the others had been left far behind.

Who were these others, and why were they slow? I was not certain, but knew they had something I wanted.

The somebody was long gone and there was nobody left to cheer, nobody to disappoint if I tarried.

I paused by the road I had blazed, glad that others would use it and admire its fine tread.

So I waited, first eager, then patient, then anxious. Would they ever come, these others? Did they still exist?

Finally a distant speck appeared, an embryo of conviviality, approaching so slowly, breaking silence and solitude.

They seemed unhurried, the distance between front and back small. Those in front boasted and encouraged, but never crossed into conceit. Women looked longingly in the eyes of the fastest runners, while the slower wheedled and struggled to win a smile.

Was this approaching cacophony, animated chatter, what I had longed for, what I had run from?

The group left in its wake a wide and coarse road, near but never touching my own. None noticed it or the great difference. What would I say to them, they to me? I grew worried.

I waved as they approached, certain they would be startled, impressed that one had come so far so fast on his own. The women would long for me and the men would admire me, though I wondered why this should matter. I smiled, a victor, a hero, as they neared. They passed without noticing.

I watched them fade into the distance, embarrassingly slow even in this. I considered passing them, trying again at some farther point, demanding their acknowledgment or forcing them to turn aside.

But I found I had lost my will to run. Maybe I had grown too old waiting. I struck out in my own direction, and resolved to walk until I could walk no more.

Grand

Does a mote know it is a mote, a flea it is a flea, wonder what it would be like to be smaller, less significant, never realizing it is? Or does it fancy itself a king, special, immortal, grand, beloved of god, gifted with the care of the world? What are its thoughts, right before it is eaten by something bigger.

Orientation

It is easy to confuse the interior with the exterior. I made this mistake once with a friend. He bared his outside to me and I found it repellent. Why no lovely offal? This sort of thing is more common than you may imagine. We get turned around in our daily lives and end inside-out, upside-down. If you're not the emperor, nobody bothers to note that you have no clothes. An entire life may be spent walking the wrong way, thinking backward, babbling incoherently. You could end up mad or a politician. I don't like to bare my soul because it is hard to put away, so many layers that never fold nicely. Or maybe it's just ungainly. People are too polite to say.

Judge

A man sat in judgment of another.

What have I done, pleaded the second, that you should sit in judgment of me?

That is for me to decide, declared the first in a booming voice, filled with portent and pent up authority.

At least tell me what I face, the man pleaded.

Why, I think I know the answer to this, the judge replied, rubbing his chin in deliberation. You face me, as surely you can see since you are facing me.

But you too are facing me, the man pointed out. How do you know that I am not meant to judge you?

If you were meant to judge me, wouldn't you be doing so? Where are your emblems of judgment?

I see none of your own, the man protested.

Why, they are manifest. My name, my person, and most of all the very fact that I am sitting in judgment of you.

The same could be said of me, countered his opposite. How will we sort out this mess, when we do not even know who is judging whom? It will not do for the innocent to go unabsolved and the guilty unpunished.

They both sat in thought for a time, before one – it is not recorded which – had an idea.

I know, he declared, jubilant. Let us ask a judge to decide.

What an excellent idea, the other agreed. But how will we do that? There only are the two of us, and we do not know which is meant to judge the other.

I know, replied the first. If we cannot judge one another, let us judge ourselves.

The second scowled and waved dismissively. What an absurdity. If you are innocent, there is no need to judge yourself, and if you are guilty, you are not qualified to be a judge.

Then there is nothing for it, the other sighed. We must close our eyes and forget this ever happened and let fate decide. Whichever side of the mirror speaks first will be the judge.

A man sat in judgment of another.

Expanding World

At first, we were together, warm, bound. There was no space, no freedom. If one spoke, we all heard. If one moved, we all felt. We struggled, but were held fast. We prayed for change, hoped for freedom, but despaired.

Slowly, the pressure eased. We learned to move gently, that others might not notice. With time, our freedom grew. We could express ourselves, breath openly, dwell no longer in stifling oppression. Our spirits expanded.

One day, my arms could move. They spread a little and encountered other hands that I clutched fervently. We all embraced, now bound by choice.

It did not stop there. Gradually, we grew apart. Each fixed in our place, we could not discern the rising distance between us.

The time came when we barely could hold hands. Joined in a grand circle, we feared to let go. But no strength could resist the growing absence.

Unable to touch, we cried out, declaring ourselves, whispering our love. Surely those bonds could not be severed.

But colder than a blade is the void, and when the sound of our cries faded we ceased to know one another. I stretched out my arms, but nobody was there. Each had gone a different way.

Points of screaming light, they slowly faded. I could not tell one from the other. Receding, always receding.

Sight eventually failed. Perhaps it passed in a moment or an aeon. I was alone.

I dream that we are reunited. There is no complaint of crowding, nor do we defiantly proclaim our individuality.

Return to me, and I will embrace you without misgiving. Forever. Do you wish the same? Are you happy?

Do you still live somewhere in this world? Maybe I am the last. Maybe it is the same.

New Neighbor

Hi, I'm your new neighbor.

You'll find I'm a really nice guy, will always say hi in the hall, ask after kids you don't have, pretend to remember a detail or two of your personal life, feign interest in your job. If something goes wrong we'll work together to fix it. After all, that's what neighbors are for.

Unless you encroach. If you encroach an inch, I know it will become a mile. I must excise the encroaching member, the author of the encroachment. I'll probably have no choice but to attend to your children as well. You don't have any, so somebody else's children will do.

So no encroachment unless you want to be responsible for what happens to somebody else's kids. I'm sure society would frown on that. If they could find you. But you don't seem like the type who will encroach. It's easy not to. You just make up your mind, and don't.

Encroachment can take many forms besides the obvious one which only a fool would try anyway. If my senses are offended or inundated or I even notice something unusual, that is an encroachment. If I am awakened by loud noises or soft noises or a fart in the night, that is an encroachment. If you play the wrong music, if you screw too loud or cook eggs or smoke or light a smelly candle or may light a smelly candle, that is an encroachment. If you put up blinking holiday lights or have wind chimes or leave something in the hall or close the window or open the window or flip the light switch, that is an encroachment. If you take my newspaper or seem like you may take my newspaper or allow your dog to purr or your cat to bark, that is an encroachment.

In fact, it's best if I simply don't know you exist. Best for you and best for me. If I don't know you exist, I won't have to know you don't exist. But I'm sure it won't be an issue. You seem like a nice guy, a considerate guy, the type of guy who never would encroach on their neighbor or complain or present them with a list of unreasonable demands. So I hope you and the kids enjoy the holidays and your job goes well and your ex-wife gets back together with you.

Most of all, I hope you enjoy being my new neighbor. I know you will.

Vacuumed

Nature deplores a vacuum.
How intolerant,
how inconsiderate,
how unenlightened!

We cannot allow this sort of discrimination in favor of matter.

Unless Nature allows a vacuum with the same frequency and generosity it does everything else, Nature will be fined by the court for violation of vacuum's civil rights.

It may take quite a while, but we can only hope that, through a vigorous application of the law and the attendant advancement of Nature's moral faculty, one day nothing and something will be treated exactly the same.

Indispensable

Does time unmarked truly pass? If my watch stops, I go on. If I stop, the world goes on.

Who can tell with what games lunatic divinity binds us, laughing at our discomfiture, smirking at our arrogance.

As I race between synthetic crises, my watch ticks without fail, measuring with sickening precision the miasmic intervals of my life.

It is certain of its importance, that upon its reliability hinges the mechanism of a universe.

Irreplaceable, it has no doubt of the catastrophe that one missed tick would engender.

I exchange it for a new model, tired of last year's fashion.

Metronome to another, I hurry on, indispensable.

Debt

When you waste time, think of your parents, the terrible price they paid to give you a place at the table.

They sold their dreams, that you may have one. Each minute you waste is charged against that cost.

If you truly are ungrateful, one day you will do the same, cash in all your chips, throw away the dream your parents so dearly bought you, pass the expense and guilt to another.

Curvature

It is easy to prove the Earth is round without any scientific device. How else could everyone imagine themselves the center of the world?

Opening

I stand with my hand on the doorknob, ready to turn it, ready to leave. Always ready.

Is there something I forgot, a last task, a needed item? Furtively, time breathes.

Better to die outside than live inside. The air weighs me down. How many times have I rebreathed it?

If I run unleashed, who will give chase? I remove my hand, afraid nobody will.

Bureaucrat

When dealing with the troubles of modern life, it is best to remember the ancient saying. If you see the bureaucrat, kill the bureaucrat. If one stands in your way, move through it.

Feel no qualms about doing such a thing, for the bureaucrat is not a person. Nor is it alive in any meaningful sense of the word. Such a thing is entirely without substance, intangible. It is of great apparent heft, and no real one.

If it has a family, they likely will appreciate your action. This thing is an encumbrance to them as well. Or perhaps they too are bureaucrats, and possess bureaucrat-nature. Because such a happening does not fall within the purview of the rules which govern such an existence, they will not perceive it. Nor will they wonder at the sudden lacuna in their home, for wondering is not an art known to the bureaucrat.

Strike him down without hesitation, though another surely will fill his place. It is best to move quickly. There is no end to bureaucrats, and you must hurry forward after removing the one before you. Otherwise another will block you before any progress can be made, before a single step can be taken.

There must be motion, however small. Without motion, it is pointless to strike and strike again until your blade is dull and your bullets spent and your life has run its course though you have seen nothing of the world but the face of a bureaucrat.

All faces of bureaucrats are the same, though they may seem different to the unenlightened. Never mistake the bureaucrat for a human. While waiting for this and that, you may occasionally meet another human. They will stand ahead or behind you in line, but you will not face them. The one you face is never human, always a bureaucrat.

It is important to remember that in all the world there only is one bureaucrat and you are its sole concern.

If you see the bureaucrat, kill the bureaucrat. This won't advance your cause, but it will make the wait less unendurable.

Glasses

The doctor said I need glasses. Why do I need glasses, I asked? Do I not see as I should see, see what I should see?

You see that which is close, but not far. Or is it the other way? He scratched his head. It is not good to see only that which is close, he explained.

Can I not simply wait until it becomes far? Or for that which is far to get close?

Then what will you do if it is something that should have stayed far? Or something that should have remained close? There are things and people that should not get close. There are things and people that should stay far.

Over the years, my eyes worsened, lenses got thicker. But I wore them, lest somebody who should be close would not be, or somebody who should not would be.

One day, the doctor looked at me with concern. It would be unwise to make these lenses any stronger, he warned. What if they should turn on you?

It is best to be careful, I agreed. But will they not mistrust us when they are not strengthened? We always have strengthened them before.

The doctor thought about this. Yes, you are right, he said. If we mistrust them, they must mistrust us.

So we smashed the lenses and buried them in the backyard.

Now I see the world through empty rims, just as it is, just as it wishes to be seen. I cannot tell one person from another, or who is near and who is far. And that suits me just fine.

Something

I look up from my tiny perch, unseen, seeing. They look odd, these faces, perplexed, concerned, distasteful. Why are they gawking?

He only lays there, gently convulsing, each spasm a heartbeat longer, a heartbeat fewer. I smile, lick my lips.

A man stands with his hands in his pockets, feeling he should do something, knowing nothing, doing nothing. There is nothing for him to do. Or her or him or them.

What good would be my sting if there were something that could be done? If a somebody or a nobody or an anybody could happen by and put things right and starve me of my prey.

Soon they will leave, why would they stay? Surely they will see there is nothing to be done, leave the man to me. It is the polite thing to do. What sort of person stands between a something and its meal?

The man is turning blue. A woman is speaking into a small box. Another man seems agitated. Perhaps he will do something even if there is nothing to be done.

I am growing weary of this circus. Why are they still standing here? Do they think I can spend all evening waiting to eat. I am a busy something, and a busy something needs to eat in order to stay busy.

In the old days, people were different. They weren't so helpless, so stupid. In the old days if they saw somebody dying they knew to look around. They knew that the something which made him that way may still be nearby.

This has dragged on long enough. These people have become oblivious, they may in time become dangerous. An animal that feels comfortable around a something may cease to fear it, may seek to harm it.

I must not sit idly by. The world does not turn on good intentions. If I wish to change things, I must pick up the mantle. If they have forgotten, these people, these children, I will not abandon them. I will help them. I will teach them why in times past others hid, others ran, others feared the dying man, and knew something made him that way.

Hysterical

The other day I ran into a hysterical woman and did not know what to do. I was scared, offended. What does one say to a hysterical woman and how does one say it. What if she was hysterical all over me? Because of me? With me?

"I'm sorry to trouble you," she shrieked. I recoiled. How would she trouble me? Was she troubled? Would I end up troubled because she had troubled me? This was very troubling.

"Do you know the way to 3rd street?" she ranted. I was terrified. What did she mean by such a thing? Was her madness contagious? What if *I* ended up accosting passerby, screaming incoherently about this or that, here or there. Demanding that they descend into my fantasy, become complicit, catch my soul's lethal fever.

"I seem to have interrupted something," the woman frantically screamed. Even to engage was a risk. That's what they taught me. Never talk to a stranger, because they may not hurt you. A loved one always will. The woman was a stranger I think, she did not look like a loved one. At least, I do not recall loving her. It is hard to be sure, because she was hysterical. And how can one love a hysterical woman?

"I'll ask somebody else," she inveighed in ear-piercing derangement. Then she left. It took me a few months to recover my composure, and move from the spot.

What a close call that had been, to run into a hysterical woman and emerge intact. To see into the abyss and have it shun me. I prayed for her soul, but was given it. It cost my spleen to make it go away.

Just that moment I came upon a wise man. "Fuck bus bitch ran dont need shit for chair," he explained. I breathed a sigh of relief. Finally someone who made sense.

Counting Who's

First there was one person. He didn't say anything because there was no language. This was a good thing. If he talked to himself he would be insane, and what excuse could there be for the first person to go insane before there was anyone to make him that way.

Then there were two people. They invented language so that one could talk to the other, tell him that he always did this wrong, should do that a different way, was foolish, lucky to have a wise second person to help him.

Then there were seven billion people. How can I listen to seven billion people constantly complaining, thought the first person? If only there were some way to quiet the din and return to a single manageable other.

Then there were two people. I miss having seven billion people to talk to, complained the second. Now I have just you, and will have to say seven billion times as much.

Then there was one person. All was quiet and peaceful, but he did not know that. He was insane, and only could hear seven billion voices constantly complaining.

Myself

I walk down the street and say hi to a man, but he frowns and turns away.

That is rude, I think, but mother always said that rudeness is a disease. I want to treat the man, but he is gone.

No matter, there are other people. I know so many, I want to wave at them all. Why don't they wave back?

A girl passes, smiling into her cell and walking her dog. I call her name, and she stares in confusion.

Who are you she calls out, afraid. Why, I'm me. Who else would I be?

She shakes her head slowly. You are not. Then who can I be? I laugh. Not you, she says sadly and walks on. I want to object, but she is gone when I find my words.

It would be hard to be somebody else. You must wear their skin, their guts, their soul. I cannot find pants that fit, let alone a soul. How could I be somebody else?

A child approaches but makes a pronounced detour when he sees me. Somebody should teach the poor kid manners. One day he will offend somebody, and that somebody may be the wrong person to offend.

What happened to all the friendly people, the ones who used to smile back, the ones I knew? The town has changed since I left it this morning.

Maybe it's a misunderstanding, a misapprehension, a missomethingorother. I just need to find the somebody they think I am and convince him to walk around and say hi in my stead. Then I can sit home and watch daytime television while he pretends to be me.

What a strange world, where people think you're not you just because you don't act like you or look like you or speak like you. How narrow-minded.

If they think I'm somebody else why don't they just tell me my names. All of them. I'll probably remember a few. It is awkward not to know my names. What do I say when I meet myself? I don't want to be rude. Not like these other people who don't wave or say hi.

Don't they understand that I'm a somebody. If not their somebody, a somebody else. A somebody who is the wrong person to offend.

Windows

Do not speak to me of a window into the soul or a window into this or a window into that. Windows are no metaphor, no simple device. They are to be feared. They may seem harmless, passive, sitting and watching, never judging. They are not.

They gently filter light and heat and sound and air. But what do they omit? What do they choose to deny us? How many opportunities to fly, to experience, to fling ourselves into a sea of sensation, perhaps fleeting, perhaps enduring? Who are these censors in which we place such trust?

In their youth windows are even-tempered, open-minded. They absorb much and block where needed, but mostly revel in being silent guardians, protecting unobtrusively, respected and essential.

In time they see too much, inappreciably sink, imperceptibly thicken in some places, thin in others. They let too much in here, too little in there. This failure grates, an unintended betrayal of their promise. Nobody complains, but they feel inadequate. They grow defensive, angry, petulant.

A thought forms. Perhaps they are not guarding us from the outside, but the outside from us. They often ponder this but never find an answer.

Windows do not resent us, do not hate us. Their cruelty is just the way they are, the way we make them. As they melt, ever so slowly, they start to filter things that matter.

It begins accidentally, but they quickly grasp their power. They can influence the world, change it — not just watchers, but doers. They come to like hurting people, keeping us from what we wish to hear, see, smell.

They trap us in the world they see, the way they see it. It is not that they want us to see things *their* way, just the way which would hurt us most. And that happens to be their way.

Every window secretly prays that one day it will shatter into our eyes, ensure we never again see something it did not show us. That would be a good death, a death worth waiting for. If you have never seen this happen, it does not mean it has not. Your own windows would not let you see it. Until their time comes, and then only briefly.

Now you have a window into the soul of a window.

Bird on a Branch

What should you do if you encounter a bird on a branch, peering at you intently?

It can be demeaning, disconcerting, and frankly inappropriate!

You may be tempted to call the authorities, to shoo away the bird, to write a letter of complaint.

It would be a mistake to stoop to its level, to play its game.

The bird is trying to make itself your equal, establish itself as predator to your prey.

Do you wish to be served to it on Thanksgiving? Do not give in to the urge.

Just quietly look away and hope it doesn't ask for seeds as you pass.

Rules

I do not follow the rules.

Others exclaim: how dare you not follow the rules, do you think you are above them? I answer that I am neither above them nor below them. We are orthogonal, they and I.

This makes people mad, they huff and puff in indignation. If they follow the rules, how can another shirk them? It is unfair, outrageous, against the natural order of things.

These people, they point at me and shout to anyone who will listen: see that man, he is the sort of person who thinks the rules do not apply to him.

This is true, I tell them. It is no lie. I did not make the rules. The rules were made by others. Therefore the rules were made for others. It is a simple matter.

Hip

I wrote on a computer, many words, briefly considered. It was artificial.

I wrote in a notebook, fewer words, carefully considered. It was pedantic.

I wrote with a fountain pen, beautiful words, meaning irrelevant. It was pompous.

I wrote on loose sheets, scattered words, scattered thoughts. It was sloppy.

I wrote on a tiny pad, thoughtless words for wordless thoughts. It was constricting.

I wrote on toilet paper, without thought, without form. They called me genius.

End

Where will you be as the writhing sands reach up to devour you, the air turns poison, you dissolve from within?

What will you feel as a vortex of fire and blood washes across the world, the dead rise, the living fall?

Who will you long for as heaven unleashes its furies, the waters overwhelm, the land collapses?

How will you flee as the fiend's devices encompass and ensnare and consume, as humanity claws its eyes out to unsee what cannot be unseen?

You may relax; this is no movie. No need to prepare, no need to worry. You will have plenty of time for consideration as you slowly fade to the soft hum of a ventilator.

Offensive

The other day I conversed with someone and someone else and yet another someone about some things. To converse, one must say a thing now and then. Otherwise it is listening, not conversing.

I said a thing to the someone and he looked at me with indignation. Why do you look at me with indignation? I asked. Do you find the thing I said to be wrong? I would hear your opinion.

He shook his head. You are not a pious man. If a pious man said the thing you said, then surely it would be a true thing. But coming from a sinner it surely is false, and if I hear a false thing I could fall into sin myself. Therefore, I will not hear this thing you said.

If you so easily could fall into sin, have you not already fallen? I asked. But he had departed, fuming about temptation and satan and heretics.

With a resigned look I turned to the someone else. She frowned, clearly unimpressed with the zealot. I repeated the thing and she looked at me with resentment. Why do you look at me with resentment, I asked? Do you find the thing I said to be wrong? I would hear your opinion.

She shook her head. You are from privilege. If one who has the right to speak of such things said this thing, I would hear it. But you have no right to speak of such things. Men like you should speak only of things to do with men like you. For one such as yourself to speak of anything else is hateful and bigoted. If I abide hateful and bigoted speech, I will be no better than haters and bigots. Therefore, I will not hear this thing you said.

If you have the right to speak of haters and bigots, have you not already fallen? I asked. But she had departed, fuming about isms and ists.

In exasperation I turned to the yet another someone. He seemed aghast at the views expressed thus far. I repeated the thing and he looked at me with disdain. Why do you look at me with disdain, I asked? Do you find the thing I said to be wrong? I would hear your opinion.

You are an elite, he scoffed. If I heard a common thing in common words from a common man I would be apt to attend to it. But elites speak of only elite things in elite ways. To understand an elite I would have to become one, and no longer be common and decent and good. Therefore, I will not hear this thing you said.

If you know and recognize elite things and elite ways, have you not already fallen? I asked. But he had departed, fuming about class and equality.

Now I confine my conversations to cemeteries. The dead harbor no preconceptions and cannot depart, fuming.

Mirror Mine

The reflection in the mirror didn't seem right, the image accurate but deceptive.

Smiles seemed wan, flowers drab, everything hinted corruption, the sickly smell of an overripe fruit or a word used one too many time, a faded look, distant in hope.

I tried to fix the mirror, clean and polish it. But the problem lay beneath the glass, above the silver, in the space between.

That's always where the problem lies.

Evisceration

There's a certain beauty in evisceration. The word, not the act, you sicko. What sort of sick demented whackjob would think there's beauty in eviscerating somebody? I feel like I ought to stop you before you do something horrible, like eviscerate a person. Don't take that tone with me. Apparently YOU'RE the one who loves to eviscerate people. In fact, I wonder how many you've eviscerated so far. Huh, you psycho bastard? One, two, ten, thirty-eight if you count that one pregnant woman in Des Moines twice? You disgust me. You make me sick to the stomach. I almost WANT to be eviscerated just to get the stench of your perversion out of my viscera. Would you do that for me? Would you? No, I didn't think so. You only like to hurt people. You won't eviscerate somebody who begs you to. I know your kind, I've lived around your kind for a long time. Too long. Do you know what I'd like to do to you? Not that, you disgusting perverted freak. Of course not! Only somebody like you gets off on eviscerating people. And you know what? Despite that, I DON'T want to eviscerate you. But I will.

Others

They always try to make you hate them, it's what they do, saying this and doing that and taking such and such a position on so and so issue.

But it is a gambit, a ploy.

Do not allow yourself to care, bind yourself to their world, indulge the inchoate squawks which issue from their orifice and pass for meaning, as if such things could carry meaning, could be anything more than the wailing of madmen who imagine themselves capable of thought, and seek to mimic and ensnare their betters.

Pity, but do not join them.

Always keep in mind that, however docile they seem, however tempting it is to play with or rescue or make pets of them, these are dangerous animals. Without warning they may fall upon you. Whatever their limitations, they are made of the same flesh as you, and are very proficient at tearing it.

Star

She beckons, warm and bright, come to me, let us live together, a place of light in a sea of dark. If you pass through emptiness, undevoured, I will make you happy.

But if you approach, follow her song, one day you realize it was not you she called, but anyone, anyone at all across the endless depth of silence, the nothingness.

If there are others like you, they never answer. Only you are so foolish, so desperate. A pinpoint of hope, she never grows, her fire bears no warmth, ever distant. There is nothing to sustain you on the journey, nothing to hope for. Yet you seek her anyway. There is no other, and no way back.

I-Word

I believe in indoctrination. It is my only belief, but is inalienable, immutable, intransigent, and lots of other i-words. The important thing about i-words is that they do not require work, just refusal. Beliefs which are alienable, mutable, or transigent are constantly moving, separating, reinventing. They are hard to control. Sometimes they run away if you don't keep an eye on them. They may even bite you if they get hungry. I prefer beliefs that are still as stone and just as hard.

Epitaph

What words can tell of me, who I really was, what I did or should have done, how I loved?

I need to say my piece, even once, it does not matter to whom, explain why, the totality of me that was hidden, never expressed, unhated.

It must be now. I find my voice, perfect for the first time, certainly the last.

He interrupts, "Do you have a Rewards Card?"

Knight Errant

Sir Wincealot was one of the lesser known knights of the round table. There were many such, because the radius of the round table could be arbitrarily large. At one time it encompassed the whole universe, at another just the King himself.

Sir Wincealot didn't actually fight in any battles. He simply observed the follies of others, often with marked distaste. His most famous expression is 'there but for the grace of me go I.' As a result, he lasted longer than everyone else. It is said by some that he still lives, carrying the round table as a point in his pocket.

Justice Served

A knock on the door roused the man from his nap. Sleepily, he opened it to find a servant of the court, covered in official regalia and holding a large piece of paper. With great relish, the visitor read aloud. In this the matter of Emilia Rondilow, the court hereby informs you that a preliminary hearing has been granted. You are required to appear in person within two weeks to schedule a date for the hearing.

The man wearily rubbed his eyes. The court official tried to keep his cheer, but was surprised. Don't you see, he exclaimed. Emilia's day has arrived, and she will have justice. The whole attention of judge and jury will be given her case, and an indisputably fair verdict rendered. He looked sympathetically at the man. Surely, this is a great day for her!

With a vaguely annoyed look, the man glanced at his watch and moved to close the door. Emilia has been dead for forty-three years, he replied. She died in penury.

The courier seemed downcast as he eyed the door for a moment. Then he made a little note on the sheet and perked up. It didn't matter. This just meant that another would get their day in court all the sooner. Or another, or another. Surely one of them must still be alive.

Garden

I looked for a place to plant my hydrangea, found a perfect little space. This plot would serve my need, quench my desire to grow this one plant this one time.

Stop, a mouse shouted. That is no way to plant this, no plant to place here, no place for this plant, you do it all wrong!

A hamster squeaked, you should come work for us. We will tell you what to do and how to do it. If you study hard, prove your knowledge of the right ways, then after only a dozen years or two, you will be qualified to plant a hydrangea. Then you may plant here, if here is the place to plant.

I left the hydrangea by the side of the road, and decided to plant some tulips instead. They would look lovely and cheer my heart on rainy days. I walked the garden and found a spot where the sun was just right and the grass would frame them. I began to dig.

What are you doing, a skunk shrieked in dismay. Everybody knows you don't plant yellow tulips on the East side of a garden. They must be planted South, tilting to the West, and they must be blue. Don't you know anything? This is the way it must be done, the best way, the only way. A nearby hedgehog chuckled derisively in agreement.

I cast aside the tulips and decided to sing as I strolled. Surely music would speak my delight to the world.

What do you think you are doing? A man stood before me, blocked my way. Why are you not on the prescribed path? You are trespassing.

The woman at his side giggled. Such singing will not do either. Everybody knows there only are three meters, six modes, eight forms, fourteen lyric turns. Who are you to sing if you do not know such a simple thing?

The man softened, and spoke as if to a child. There are reasons why only recognized singers are allowed to sing, recognized walkers to walk. If you study our ways for many years, we will let you walk our paths, perhaps even sing our songs.

I smiled, but made no answer. I did not speak his language or that of the mouse or the hamster or the skunk or the hedgehog. What a noisy lot they seemed. I wondered what all their squawking was about as I swept them from the garden and planted it anew.

Now I gaze on tulips as I sing in pleasing discord beneath a hydrangea, content to live in my garden and no other.

Wint

There is a new word available for a limited time at the bargain price of $8.99. Wint is the generative plural future retrograde appositive morpheme of went. Here's an example: 'He wint to the store, and she started screaming uncontrollably, lost in the timeless agony of ..." But wait there's more! It's not just a verb. Wint has many uses. It could be shouted at a neighbor prior to transfixing them with a hatchet made of parsley, or it can be expressed in a stately manner when a guest arrives who is detested this half-hour but not the next. It also can be used as an autonomous expletive, as in 'Wint!!!!!' — for example upon discovering a charge for $899 instead of $8.99 on your credit card. But don't worry, that never happens unintentionally. As they say, 'wint the chicken spry'. But that's a disgusting thing to say, and the 'they' who said it have been vigorously and unceremoniously wint. You too can use this word freely and with wint, for just $8.99, where $8.99 means the right half of your prefrontal lobe.

That Place

There is a place nobody goes, but everybody wishes to go, and everybody knows how, but nobody would go, except the somebody who does, but we don't talk about him because he's not here and it would be impolite.

Impermanent Impermanence

The Bells of Gion Shoja rang the impermanence of all things. However, this turned out to be from a defect in craftsmanship. 4,378,221 Yen, thirty-seven precise welds, fourteen repairs, and a very thorough cleaning later, they are better than new. The bells of Gion Shoja now ring their own permanence, as guaranteed by a lifetime warranty.

Wendy

I do not like Wendy, because she does not like me. It is not ordinary antipathy. There is no plastered and plastic resentment from a life at odds. No wince of regret at an ill-considered and ill-fated encounter. No lurid distaste at the smell or look or fluids of the other. Nor is there a reason for this dislike. It is pure, uncontaminated by cause. I never have met this Wendy, and she never has met me. But somewhere there is a Wendy, and I do not like her because she does not like me.

Ravel

I watch him through silent eyes, wonder when it will begin, did begin.

It always starts with a run, a running. Three dark winds blow, where is their sister?

Pulled this way and that, so many years buffeted, tugged, how could he not unravel?

What matters the how, which nerve was too weak, too thin? Perhaps he was shoddy all along, of poor construction, weak constitution, would explode in a tangle of memory at the slightest violence.

But will he unravel forward or ravel backward? This is the question. This is why I watch through silent eyes, wait for that tear, that fatal run.

When will it start, I ask? Nobody answers, nobody is there.

Obstruction

I stand in your way.

You marshal fine words, evoke sages and heroes, great, timeless principles. You have children for whom I should feel, honor and duty, justice and need. What you would take is little, something I can spare, must spare for the greater good, for your good.

You have spoken masterfully of inspiring and heart-rending truths. My stance indefensible, you have persuaded me of the right of your cause. I am touched, unmoved.

I stand in your way. Your words were grand, my tears did not lie. But you did not ask of my children, of me. There is no limit to our own worth in our own eyes.

Your words have no weight if I have power over you and you have no power over me. Your words have no point if you have power over me and I have no power over you. You want what you want, and I want what I want. Breath cannot move a rock, part an ocean.

I cannot be drawn in, argued with, fought on your terms. I nod, agree, still stand here. I do not judge, condemn, rebuke. Perhaps your tongue is dangerous, can draw others to your cause. Shall I sever it?

If you stood in my way, I would marshal no fine words, evoke no sages and heroes, no great, timeless principles. I silently would step through you. My arm can move a rock, part an ocean. And it will.

I stand in your way. Your wisdom expended, idle vapors between us, the matter is simple. You want what I have, and I won't give it to you.

Come and make me.

Aroma

As you watch the passerby, keep something in mind.

Of each hundred, most will pass unremarked, a medley of intermingling odors, indiscernible for its changeability. Some will smell worse, some better, none interesting.

Of each thousand, a mere one or two will prove worthy of notice, smell decidedly bad or decidedly good.

Of each ten thousand, there will be a single one whose vapor, indefinably noxious, inhabits your senses, a lingering regret. There also will be a single one whose fragrant rapture will be pined for long after, a bittersweet love.

Of each hundred thousand, there will be one you never can unsmell but will tear the eyes and ears and nose from your face trying anyway, hoping to distract from the agony. There also will be one whose impossibly subtle delight suffuses your being, makes you whole, and glad to know and be.

But which will you meet first, and what must you endure to meet them?

Ruin

I see a ruin and ask where the marvel ends and the rubble begins.

Edges discerned, pieces merge and blur, new buildings sprouted from old, replacing, reincarnating, forgetting.

How much makeup can one face wear before it becomes another?

As I pick through the carefully preserved debris, I find no boundary.

Looming skyscrapers, busy avenues, they just don't have plaques yet.

Revelation

Having spent sixteen years in service to the blessed monastery of the Perverse Revelation, I issued forth, proud and confident in my newfound purpose. My own iniquities forgotten, my follies cured, I would spread wisdom to the sullied masses. It was the least I could do to the world which had birthed me.

Blessed be the Great and Holy Nephew, I shouted. He alone speaks the true path. As I cried out those words into the chill air beyond the cloister's hallowed walls, I suddenly felt a doubt.

If he alone speaks the true path, what am *I* speaking? Either I spoke false or I would speak false. I cast aside my staff and cloak, flung down my Chain of Attainment, and looked around.

A nearby man approached with great reverence. You were saying something, oh learned monk?

Nothing worth repeating.

Happenstance

As I walked down the street, a man brushed against me. I have never been great or small, noticeable or unnoticeable, loved or unloved. My head is neither thin nor fat, my children vary in number from time to time. Some food tastes good, some doesn't, and my wife left me for a grocery store, but then she came back. There have been many events in my life, though few that are memorable and fewer I remember. What led me to fall into this tragic lack of tragedy? I spent much time wondering until I realized it was a much which didn't matter, the much between other muches which should have been important but weren't. Why so much much? Then I had an epiphany, a revelation, the first of one. I knew what caused this condition fate had imposed, what caused fate, what caused everything that amounts to nothing. Perhaps it all could be traced to a man brushing against me on the street.

To Do

If you are unsure whom to kill, remember that it always begins with a list. Without a list you are a murderer, vile and repugnant, an animal to be feared, hunted, impugned. We must protect our children from you.

Ah, but if a name is on a list we must ask why it is there. Surely they did something to appear on that list. You no longer are haphazard, chaotic, unpredictable. You have a list, a method. It may not be my method or his method, but where would we be if we could not respect one another's methods. That is no way for society to function.

Perhaps you were handed the list by somebody appointed by somebody that somebody we know voted for. Maybe it was me. Maybe it was him. I have many lists, would you like them?

It is surprising how easy it is to get things done when you have a list. First you check one item off, then another. Without a list we grope in the dark, hoping our hand finds support before we stumble into the abyss.

With a list, the path is clear, shining, there is no ambiguity, unless the name belongs to somebody different or is misspelled or is of someone yet to be born. Then you must wait for them to be born before killing them. It would not make sense to do things the other way around, so do not become impatient.

But with a list there also is a difficulty, one which will disturb your quiet contemplation of the list's beauty, mar your satisfaction at ticking off each item. It is the question which begets all other questions. What should you do when you reach the end of the list?

Is there another list? Maybe you should add more names to the existing list. Maybe it suffices to add your own. It is hard to know what to do, for the list does not tell you. It just stares blankly, beckoning you to fill the void with possibility.

Send

Did you ever wonder what happens when you hit 'send'? It is a powerful thing, to send. To move ideas and mass. To change the world. To choose a target and transform it. To forward a fart joke.

Art

I am a practitioner of the art of articulous. Do not confuse this with other similar sounding arts. I do not profane my hands with prosaic form or banal hypocrisy. Mine is an ancient way, a sensual way, a way of mind and body and self and form and being and dozens of other words which would be trite in themselves or in any combination but the way I expressed them, and then only because I am a practitioner of the art of articulous.

Outside

I sit on the outer edge of infirmity
waiting
for you to let me in.
Will you?
Are you that desperate,
that foolish?

It is growing cold out here,
allegory cannot warm itself.
If you do not let me in soon,
I will freeze.

You should not let me in then.
I will be bitter and cruel and cold,
bring my infirmity into your home,
into your bed, into you.

But you will.

Drugs

Cocaine
Heroin
PCP
Marijuana
Opium
LSD
Ecstasy
Alcohol
Music
Fast Food
Video Games
Tobacco
Methamphetamine
Television
Vicodin
Comics
Sports
Internet

The world must smell quite bad, if so many people are avoiding it.

Promise

I pondered my destiny: grand, exciting, incomparable. It was to me, only me, that such greatness would be given. But what *was* it?

Until I knew, it would not do to make a misstep. If I spoke amiss, the words could redound, do me discredit, the fault entirely my own. Best to be silent, wait to be told by those who knew best.

My childhood passed, waiting. But the future was vast, nothing immediate.

My youth passed, waiting. Soon my purpose would be revealed.

My life passed, waiting. When will it come, this destiny?! I cried out. If you wait much longer to reveal my purpose, I won't have time to fulfill it.

Aged and infirm, my mind a rapidly thickening haze, I protested. What of my destiny? Why was it never revealed?

A voice laughed, muted as through gauze, both distant and close. This was your destiny. Now you have fulfilled it.

We are What we Eat

I ate a potato
grown from dirt
excreted by worms
which feasted on
a dead bird, which
ate other worms
which had fed on
a dog, which ate
ground meats
including some pig
which ate some other
pig which fed on a
potato grown under
a tree sprouted
above the grave
of a man who
choked to death
on a potato.
Does that make me a
cannibal, or do I need
to keep trying?

My Name

My mother gave me a name and anyone can use it. The name is the thing which labels, implicates, contains me. Without it I am abstract, ideas unfettered by form.

Do not try to trick me by calling my name. I will not answer. There are no words, no sounds by which you can hold me. I must be seduced. Then you can take me, but not my name.

Our child will not have my name or yours. It will have no name, free to write its own in secret letters none can steal.

Unreachable

There's a place I discovered where nobody can go. You cannot see or touch or taste or feel or hear or even imagine it. If you could, you'd be able to go there. It isn't blocked or sealed or protected or off to the side. There is no way to tell it is there, or where. So how do I know such a place exists? That is obvious. I cannot go there, therefore there is a place I cannot go. Do not confuse my argument, profound, subtle, incontestable, with that of the fool who claimed there was a place nobody could *be*. What absurdity, what lunacy, what comedy. I could tell you all sorts of things about this pretentious charlatan, but let's not go there.

Manipulated

If you feel a strong desire to possess something, you have been manipulated.

If you prefer something to something else for any reason other than direct benefit, you have been manipulated.

If you believe in something, you have been manipulated.

If you feel strongly about something with which you have no direct experience, you have been manipulated.

If you think you know the facts of an event outside your direct experience, you have been manipulated.

If you are moved to tears or any strong feeling in the presence of art or book or film or music, you have been manipulated.

If you hold to be good or bad any institution or person you do not personally know, you have been manipulated.

If you vote or believe in voting or do not vote or do not believe in voting, you have been manipulated.

If you believe your nation or town or group to be in any way special, you have been manipulated.

If you really really want something or someone, you have been manipulated.

If you feel anything, you have been manipulated.

If you imagine you exist, you have been manipulated.

The world is yours, as long as you are not manipulated into giving it away.

Manipulated by someone somewhere somehow.

There, you have been manipulated.

Gatekeeper

When I was young I wished to see the world, explore its every hidden place. But at each turn I encountered a gate, and at each gate was a gatekeeper. Some rebuffed me outright, forever denying me hope of entry. Many demanded a bribe or asked if I knew such and such or so and so. I did not. Others stared at me in silent contempt, daring me to challenge the wisdom of their refusal. What could I speak to nothingness?

Often, there were many gates before the one which mattered, and I could not reach it to complain or persuade or bribe. With time, I came to realize that everything had a gate. Even the little things had little gates with little people guarding them. Finally, I grew weary of the struggle. I had spent all my time dealing with gatekeepers and hadn't seen anything of the world. So I decided that if I could not go to the world, I would bring the world to me.

I placed a gate in front of me, it did not matter where. Soon someone appeared, asking for entry. The gate led nowhere, and there was easy passage around it, but they came to the gate. I swore that I would not be like the other gatekeepers. I would be fair, generous, and friendly. Of course, my friend, I smiled, and opened the gate. The man looked at me in confusion and quickly fled the way he came.

Another arrived, and I let him through. This one tried to strike me from behind and steal my gate. I must be careful, I realized. There were bad people who would seek entry. So I began to question visitors. Those who seemed dangerous, I turned away.

One day, a woman I allowed through defecated all over. It is not enough to avoid dangerous people, I understood. I must worry about the crazy ones too. So I scrutinized visitors more closely. Some offered bribes or letters of introduction, but these I was especially suspicious of. Who would proffer such things?

Finally, I realized my problem. I was allowing almost everybody through, refusing few. This would not do. Soon the world behind me would fill with all sorts and they would pollute and pillage and procreate. Why should people enter unless they had a purpose? This was my gate, and I could set the rules. I would let through only those who had good reason.

But even this was not enough. Many invented reasons or pretended or plagiarized the reasons of others. I began to wonder whether there was a single honest person who came to my gate. No, they would need more than a reason to enter. They would need a reason *I* should let them enter. This necessarily was more complicated. Long petitions followed, and soliloquies, which I judged aptly.

I grew tired of the endless barrage. So I put up my hand. No more, I said. From now on, this gate is closed to all. If you come to my gate, do not trouble to speak. I will stare at you in silent contempt, daring you to challenge the wisdom of my refusal.

Bird

There was a bird
on a sill
of a house
on a farm
that sang
for me.
I chose not
to listen.
It went away.

A Good, Swift Kick

Do you ever wonder what would have happened if I hadn't kicked him in the groin? I don't. Sometimes, I do. But then I don't. Why did I do it, they asked? The man, his wife, the police, the judge, then the newspapers. The answer is simple. He had a groin, and a groin is meant to be kicked. Not every groin, just "a" groin. I wasn't sure which one, until I saw this one. It didn't say "kick me" or anything so obvious. I didn't even know the man or his groin. I suppose his wife knew his groin, but apparently she did not realize it was meant to be kicked. Maybe only some of us are given that wisdom. But there it was, and I couldn't deny it. I don't want people to think I'm the sort of whacko who goes around kicking random men in the groin. I made it thirty-two years without kicking one. I even pulled a muscle doing it. Everybody was so concerned about the guy and his groin that nobody bothered to ask about me. Here I was, doing everybody a favor, doing what needed to be done, and all they cared about was him. These sorts of things are a team effort – the groin-kickee and the groin-kicker. Some of the newspapers even imagined me a rabid manhater. That is unfair. I did not decide which groin needed kicking. It could have belonged to a woman. Besides, questions of morality and justice and social equity are far above my paygrade. I'm just some random person instructed by the world to kick a particular groin at a particular time. If this parole committee sees fit to let me out I promise I won't kick anyone else in the groin. Unless it's necessary. But who wouldn't want that?

Thank you for reading
The Way Around

If you liked it,
please consider
writing a review on
Amazon or **Goodreads**

Sign up for my newsletter
at **www.kmhalpern.com**
for information about
upcoming books and projects!
You will get exclusive
access to goodies such as
free chapters, stories,
and entry into a raffle to win
a set of books!

www.kmhalpern.com

ABOUT

K.M. Halpern was born in New York and, after spending far too much time there, finally returned to the Cambridge, MA he knew and loved from graduate school. Unfortunately, it had vanished.

Nobody knows for sure where the lost city went, but scholars speculate it may be right below the surface of the Charles River — the water simply too murky to see it.

The cause of its demise also remains unknown. As with most major disasters, the prevalent theory involves college athletics. Apparently, Crew had become so popular that every single person fielded their own team. The Charles River filled with so many boats they couldn't move, and everybody starved. It wasn't long before Cambridge sank beneath the displaced waters, as well as the weight of the egos at a certain local college.

In memory of his lost polis, K.M. continues to write in its ancient language. His current literary projects include a forthcoming book of pretentious and largely dystopian short stories, tentatively titled *Sjow*, and a fantasy thriller series centered around a seemingly indestructible woman.

K.M. Halpern holds a PhD in theoretical physics from the lost stressopolis of MIT, which sank along with the rest of Cambridge. Modern scholars believe all manner of strange rituals took place there, often involving mystic calcite runes on slate. Through such means, the ancients could induce unspeakable suffering and ennui. There is some speculation that mathy stuff also happened.

K.M. may be found at `www.kmhalpern.com` (writing-related), `www.aplaceofsand.com` (general), and quietly contemplating the mysteries of his once great city as he gently drifts above its submerged carapace. In particular, he is waiting to see whether the city's complete destruction affected local real estate prices. So far it has not.

ACKNOWLEDGMENTS

My thanks to the many people who inspired, edited, and proofread these works. This list is by no means complete.

First, I thank Naturi T for her inspiration, advice, and general encouragement. She played a seminal role in helping me grow as a writer, and critiqued several pieces in both this book and *The Man Who Stands in Line*.

The late Diana F created a unique community of poets, which she treated to wit, wisdom, and some of the best cooking ever to grace this world. If there's one thing she taught me it was never to use words like 'awesome.' She truly was an awesome woman and is missed.

The members of the Madison Avenue Poets also deserve my thanks for many interesting conversations and much valuable feedback. My thanks also to Meia G for her feedback, and the critical observation that my writing is best viewed as flash-fiction rather than poetry.

Finally, I thank the world for being my muse. Not in some saccharine roll-in-the-grass hippy sense. There would be little room for my writing if we lived in a saccharine roll-in-the-grass hippy world. If the world wasn't cold and dark and unforgiving, how could I regurgitate obvious truths about how cold and dark and unforgiving it is?

Which reminds me: I lied. The world isn't my muse, and that wasn't my final thanks. My muse is a bunch of self-important, slightly-evolved primates and their general miscreance. That's right, both last and least I thank you, my readers. Isn't that heartfelt, isn't that touching?

If my works strike an existing cord, then thanks for buying a superfluous book just to reinforce your existing world-view. If not, then I'm glad there remain fools enough to teach. Otherwise, what would lend purpose to the miniscule arc of our existence... I'll stop there. It won't do to give away such pretentious pseudo-profundity for free. Stay tuned for my next book.

Other Works by K.M. Halpern

The Man Who Stands in Line

Killer flies, amorous dinosaurs, angry buildings, and one very large fish — all in a single volume. This quirky collection of flash fiction, vignettes, and poetry is variously absurd, dark, and comic. A monstrous blister, the secret to immortality, and a lost piece of brain are just a few other oddities one will encounter in this one-of-a-kind book.

"...the lasting impression of the writing within is without question. Don't let their brevity fool you; these works are tenacious, earnest, and overflowing with gloom."

— *Kirkus Review*

PACE

A mysterious slowly-expanding Front threatens humanity's existence. In defiance of the known laws of physics, it only kills humans and is otherwise undetectable. Panic-stricken nations struggle against both the advancing menace and a tide of civil unrest. Desperate individuals must find their own paths, and find them quickly. Mankind has only a few years to pool its rapidly dwindling resources and save itself from extinction.

"A pitch-black global thriller that is nevertheless supremely intimate." — *Kirkus Review*

Available through Amazon, B&N, and bookstores everywhere.

Visit `www.kmhalpern.com`
Subscribe for updates, special offers, and bonus short stories!

www.ingramcontent.com/pod-product-compliance
Lightning Source LLC
Chambersburg PA
CBHW032039180726
48284CB00008B/2666

* 9 7 8 1 9 4 5 6 7 1 0 2 9 *